CHAPTERS COLLECTED TOO

BY J. TYSON

COPYRIGHT 2025 ALL RIGHTS RESERVED
PARENTS PRODUCTIONS
parentsproductions2025@yahoo.com
ISBN: 979-8-218-99373-3
UNITED STATES

THESE PAGES ARE DEDICATED
TO MY
FAMILY, FRIENDS,
NEPHEW RODNEY,
FAMILY AND FRIENDS WHO
HAVE PASSED ON
ALSO, FOR
THE FAMILY OF THE LATE
ALBERT L. PERRY
VIET NAM COMBAT VETERAN

AND

THE VERY BEST BARBER

CHAPTERS COLLECTED TOO CONTENTS
Introduction

TABLE OF CONTENTS

Chapter 1 "CELL" INTRODUCTION to 2
Chapter 2 KWOTES… 6
Chapter 3 Critical Mass 1 Introduction 33
Chapter 4 Critical Mass 2 37
Chapter 5 Critical Mass 3 40
Chapter 6 Critical Mass 4 44
Chapter 7 Critical Mass Five Caught-Up One 47
Chapter 8 "BENJI AND DAVON" 49
About The Author: 53

CHAPTERS COLLECTED TOO
INTRODUCTION
THESE CHAPTERS ARE NOT DIRECTLY RELATED TO EACH OTHER. THEY ARE SELECTED CHAPTERS FROM MY LIFE.
CHAPTER 1, "CELL," SPEAKS TO THE SOCIAL MEDIA PHENOMENON AND CELL PHONES.
CHAPTER 2, "KWOTES…" ARE 104 QUOTES ABOUT LIFE.
CHAPTERS, 3, 4, 5, AND 6 TALK ABOUT THE COVID CRISIS
CHAPTER 7 IS CONCERNED WITH AN OLD VICE MAKING A COMEBACK.
CHAPTER 8 "BENJI AND DAVON" EXPLORE
A SOCIAL PROBLEM.

"CELL"

INTRODUCTION TO CHAPTER 1

Chapter 1 reflects on the proliferation of social media and the cell phone phenomenon.
We now give you: "Cell."
On your mobile phone, it keeps you in a zone.
You rarely make a call—it keeps you in a stall.
Going forward I can't tell; all I can say is, "Oh well."
A cell can distract—time you can't get back.
Having a cell phone, for some, can make them kind of numb.
Using your memory bank won't leave you so blank.

Put the cell down while walking
around town.
While in your prime, don't waste
your time.
Looking at your phone like a dog
eyes a bone,
your hands will cramp, as your
palms get damp.
Cells can be dope and gotcha on
a rope.
Don't share a street fight—can't
you see the light?
Some videos—why watch? You
only become another notch.
Can't get good traction with cell
phone distraction.
Some people already know—cells
can make real dough.
Cells make time well Spent
with all things under one tent.

The best asset of phones called cells
can create high revenue in office tales.
Your business can soar like a moonshot rocket,
With your office in your front or back pocket.
Where change is forever consistent,
success with a cell phone is not distant.
Cell phones defined a new economy
and broke old business monotony.
Progress will always be on the move.

*Technology is here to use—
Keep abreast of trends and cruise.
Look to science—you cannot lose!*

Any comments or questions for our mental health therapist or chapter 1 back story, send us an email.

Thanks
parentsproductions2025@yahoo.com

CHAPTER 2 KWOTES

CONTENTS

Quotes 1-2 10
Quotes 3-6 11
Quotes 7-11 12
Quotes 12-19 13
Quotes 20-27 14
Quotes 28-34 15
Quotes 35-44 16
Quotes 45-51 17
Quotes 52-57 18
Quotes 58-63 19
Quotes 64-66 21
Quotes 67-74 22
Quotes 75-78 24
Quotes 79-82 26
Quotes 83-84 27

CHAPTER 2 KWOTES...
CONTENTS (CONT)

Quotes 85-90..29
Quotes 91-94..30
Quotes 95-101..31
Quotes 102-104..32

KWOTES...INTRODUCTION

I am someone who seeks practical wisdom and shares it freely, though I wouldn't call myself a philosopher. I define a philosopher (with tongue-in-cheek) as a person who has lived other lives, in other times... but won't admit it publicly.

However, such a person will gladly acknowledge having received a formal education in philosophy.

In my view, a philosopher is someone who listens intently and respectfully to their mothers, fathers, sisters, brothers, wives, husbands, friends, and relatives—and who also happens to have studied philosophy in an academic setting.

Digesting this material should be easy if one sticks to a steady diet of either total consumption or three quotes a day.

Kwotes can be read in order or at random. Dissect and absorb all interpretations. Try to align your thoughts with the quotes—to see where they fit with you, and where you fit with them.

Some of the practical wisdom in these quotes may sound familiar, echoing other well-known sayings. That's because conversations I heard at a young age—spoken by many different people—were embedded deep in my subconscious. Without any intention of plagiarism, these ideas later resurfaced in my own words.

The word love appears in many of my quotes. The kind of love I refer to is a compassionate mindset—one that extends toward all people.

Unless otherwise noted, all quotes are original.

KWOTES Quotes 1-2

1. There are three levels of physical being where you constantly grow.
There are three levels of mental existence where you constantly stow.
There are three levels of love that you should constantly show, love for family, love for life, and love for self.
2. There are three kinds of love: love for family, love for friends, and love for all people.
The common thread that runs through all three kinds of love is compassion, consideration, and companionship are what life is about and revolve around. Everyone should incorporate these threads into their lives, and there will be no room for bigotry, or hate.

Quotes 3-6

3. You can always afford the luxury of a positive idea—but you cannot afford the disruption of a negative thought.
4. Everything in and on this Earth—plants and trees that grow, and all "real" animals that walk or fly—are perfect,
except for human beings.
5. Thoughts on respect and trust: Having respect for your parent(s) can guide you to respect yourself and others. Respect builds trust. Respect and trust are the building blocks for a foundation that connects us to all of life.
6. Opposites in balance, balance the world. (Original quote from Chinese philosophy.)

Quotes 7-11

7. There is an infinite picture above, and an infinite picture below. We are part of both—together, they form the big picture.
8. The words children and sponge are synonymous, children absorb. People must take great care in both the content and context of what children absorb.
9. People have the will to survive. After conquering daily existence, the drive to improve life takes over.
10. The night is never as dark as it seems. As time passes, you begin to see more—perhaps even enough to find your way through the darkness, and if truly desired, a way out.
11. Even in darkness, there is a light you can see.

Quotes 12-19

12. You must be at peace with yourself in order to accept true happiness.
13. I have enough love for everyone— and more love for the one who loves me.
14. Best friend. Close friend. Good friend. A true friend until the end doesn't need a helping verb.
15. Friendship in marriage is marriage.
16. Expect the least and you may get the most. Expect a lot and you may get very little. (Anonymous)
17. You cannot find a friend. You cannot make someone be your friend. You can only have a friend.
18. Respect yourself, and you can respect all. Love yourself, and you can love all. (s.s.a.-should all.)
19. Life can be easygoing. Some people just make it complicated. (Anonymous)

Quotes 20-27

20. A friend in a wife is a friend for life.
21. Space, compared to the mind, is basically the same—both hold endless possibilities.
22. Loving is living—if not, you only exist.
23. Walk through your life the best you can.
24. You can do what you can... or you can do better.
25. Life can be long and enjoyable, be it short—
or life can be short and painful, be it long.
26. Enjoy the walk through your life the best you can.
27. Talk a little, do a lot.
(Anonymous)

Quotes 28-34

28. Time is never wasted.
29. For some people, time may not be filled to the fullest—
so LIVE YOUR LIFE!!!
30. Life is the way it is meant to be. To accept what you cannot change is to accept and understand life as it is presented. (Anonymous)
31. Understanding, added to loving, equals living.
32. Be kind whenever possible. It is always possible. (Anonymous)
33. Take care of your body— it's the only place you have to live. (Anonymous)
34. Friends are the people who allow you to smile brighter, laugh louder, and live better. (Anonymous)

Quotes 35-44

35. Love for love.
36. Do not love for evol (evil), for that is hate.
37. Life is too short to make it long with pain.

38. Love all who are living—
if not, you are not truly living or loving.
39. Take time out... or time will take you out.
40. Love of self is success.
41. You can watch people succeed—
or you can do better.
42. Live a fast life, and real life can pass you by.
43. Love yourself for success.
44. I am who I think I am,
a person—nothing more, and nothing less.

Quotes 45-51

45. Life is worth living—if you love while living.
46. Liking oneself and venerating everyone spells love.
47. A person is no greater than an ant and no smaller than a whale— for we are all the same: living.
48. You can have time-saving devices, you can have fast computers, but only you can give yourself peace of mind.
49. It is possible to slow the gears of a fast life to catch up with a less complex one.
50. It is better to be loved than to want to be loved— for all who love will surely be loved.
51. Love is a friend to all and an enemy to none. (Anonymous)

Quotes 52-57

52. Trouble comes and trouble goes—but love stays around for all time.
53. "It is easy to stand in a crowd, but it takes courage to stand alone."—Gandhi
54. We do not have time—time has us.
55. We should not be deep into ourselves (vanity), or deep into our lives (selfishness), but we should be deep into life.
Having respect for all of life—and for human rights—is to be responsible in life.
s.s.a.
56. If you slow your pace, when going fast is useless or unnecessary, you may find it easier to enjoy your life.
57. "In order to have friends, you must first be one."
—Elbert Hubbard

Quotes 58-63

58. For some, time passes too fast. But perhaps it's not time that's rushing—it may be you going through spans of time without stopping to smell the roses.
59. Think of something you feel good about during the day, without distracting from your work, create a smile in your mind—for yourself.
60. "You must find love within yourself; it is useless to look for love elsewhere or in anyone."
—Francois Duc de La Rochefoucauld
61. Love, in no way, hurts. It is people who place the blame on love.
62. People do not realize the perfection of love—and so they fail to examine their own faults or accept the faults in others.

*63. You cannot make a person happy.
You can only allow the person to be
happy.*

Quotes 64-66

64. This society is evolving, and more women will have careers, jobs, or businesses. At this time, ONLY women can give birth to children. Therefore, at some point, a lady may have at least one child. Regardless of when childbirth occurs—before, during, after, or between careers, jobs, or business endeavors—a woman must take some time off just before and after giving birth. Women ARE in an exclusive club. Only women can have children, and ALL women deserve ALL the respect— from everyone, always.
65. You cannot make a person love you—you can only share the love between each other.
66. Love is never lost or found— love is always around.

Quotes 67-74

67. "Knowledge is power."
—Francis Bacon
68. "The best and most beautiful things in the world cannot be seen or even touched—
they must be felt with the heart."
—Helen Keller
69. "Strong minds discuss ideas. Average minds discuss events. Weak minds discuss people."
—Eleanor Roosevelt
70. The best quality we all have in common is love.
71. "There is more to life than increasing its speed."
—Gandhi
72. Love will find love.
73. You can watch people succeed, or you can better yourself.

74. Adversity is a part of life. It must be faced and managed in order to channel the experience into a positive learning opportunity—something to draw from in future situations.

Quotes 75-78

75. There is not one test that love can fail.
76. Loving is a way of life—not just a part of life.
77. Love can be good, or love can be very good. There is never a time when love can be of no good.
78. Times will change—there have been single-parent families and blended families long before this modern era. Some people view a part of life as women having the proclivity of wanting too much. Some men with the preoccupation of having too much, and some children with the propensity of needing too much. In my observation of life, individuals with a child, children, or none, may simply wish to be with someone who meets their need for companionship.

I believe all families, in their own way, can provide an acceptable a healthy growing atmosphere (H.G.A.) by holding periodic family meetings and understand that no one is perfect-only doing their best.

Quotes 79-82

79. Some people wait for love.
Some people look for love.
All people should just... love.
80. We live in the lives of each other—with each person living a life of their own. Through all of life, we should carry love for all.
81. He, she, and they took time to show me pure love—and I have the time to give him, her, and them all my love.

82. Pure love speaks through time and space, reaching its destination without delay. It may take hours, days, or even years,
but it always arrives—at just the right moment.

Quotes 83-84

83. There are no half-loves or step-loves. Love has no timetable for reaching its highest level.
Some loves are only destined to reach a certain depth in this lifetime. Accept that—and love on.

84. In my opinion, there are no stepmothers, stepfathers, half-sisters, or half-brothers.
I prefer to refer to them as fathers, mothers, sisters, or brothers in residence. Being a mother, father, sister, or brother in residence means serving in that role model capacity for all practical purposes—regardless of when that role is realized.

In addition, boundaries and expectations should be clearly and respectfully expressed-through

*rational, adult conversations—
ideally during a family meeting.*

Quotes 85-90

85. A touch of love is needed in the here and now. Love is an ongoing flow. If you feel you've lost love—you haven't. The love you once experienced may have been shaded by situations, certain times, circumstances, or people. But love itself was never lost.
86. Life can be short. Live it long—as if one minute were a lifetime.
87. Love is long—live it short, as if one minute will pass too fast.
88. Every ounce of your being is pure love. Let it flow—and do not let it go.
89. People and circumstances can slow your flow, but pure love will let you grow.
90. Loving is easy—and always there. Hating is hard—and leads nowhere.

Quotes 91-94

91. Love can show all people peace, and peace from the heart can show all people love.
92. Peace of mind can reveal love from the heart, and love from the heart can give everyone peace of mind.
93. Love has existed for all time. Total understanding of love is beyond our comprehension.
    We should accept love as an abstract thought. In mathematical terms, love is equal to a constant— or a given.
    A constant is something accepted as always true. The proof of love being real lies in the love we accept, share, and feel.
94. Life can be easygoing if you remember the basics: respect, responsibility, and reaching out (with the intent to understand).

Quotes 95-101

95. One of the hardest parts of life is learning to let go—to pass a loved one from a physical being into a memorable, joyful essence.
96. True character stands firm—like the Rock of Gibraltar—unshaken by the winds of taste or time.
97. Love is never over—only a fresh start on a new day.
98. Love is a friend until the end... and beyond.
99. There can be peace and calm in the throes of love. Chaos and confusion often arise where love is rarely on display.
100. Pure love, real love, and true love can only grow.
101. To honestly live life is to show love at all three levels:
love for family, love for life, and love for self.

Quotes 102-104

102. "Never be limited by other people's limited imaginations."
—Mae C. Jemison

103. "Hope and fear cannot occupy the same space at the same time. Invite one of them to stay."
—Maya Angelou

104. Do the best you can until you know better.
Then when you know better, you can do better."
—Maya Angelou

Any comments or questions for our certified mental health therapist or chapter 2 back story can send us an email.
Thanks
parentsproductions2025@yahoo.com

CHAPTER 3

CRITICAL MASS 1

INTRODUCTION

Each generation had unique challenges, some greater than others. Between 1901 and 1924, World War I started, and the influenza pandemic erupted. During the next 21 years, the Great Depression and World War II occurred between 1924 and 1945. The Baby Boomers, between 1945 and 1965, saw the end of World War II and the onset of the Vietnam War. Gen X, between 1965 and 1976, saw the end of the War and the oil embargo.

Generation Y, in the 90's watched the Gulf Wars in real time.
Generation Z, in the 2000s, had 9/11 and ISIS to cope with. The generation
that graduated in 2019, I refer to them as Generation C, for the COVID-19 Crisis. We now give you,
"Critical Mass 1"
In 2020, COVID-19 put me in a guillotine right on my Nehru collar, now, some cannot make a dollar. Can't play baseball in
the snow. COVID can't care and doesn't know. Some can play in a safe bubble, mostly without the fear of COVID trouble.

COVID has been doing the most and burned businesses like toast. COVID came à la carte, without a vaccine counterpart. My mate was states away when COVID made its start. Some are not in any school. COVID can be so very cruel. With big, bold written rules stating that wearing masks are necessary tools.

In January 2020, I started my new career, now it seems so far, yet nowhere near. The virus cannot hear, but I have no shrinking fear. This too, will pass, and some effects will last. Later we'll have a blast like actors in a Broadway cast.

We will surely cope because we do

have hope. COVID is not dope, it can reach the Pope!

Depression can hit anyone, even those in "Hamilton," people in the Dominican, or those in Fort Sheridan. The absolute meaning of life is having a partner, mate, husband, or wife. For some, raising children is a choice, or not, others are left to a fateful unknown lot. Enjoy life and the best of times, good memories can make dope rhymes.

Any comments or questions for our certified mental health therapist or back story on Critical Mass 1 can send us an email.

Thanks

parentsproductions2025@yahoo.com

CHAPTER 4

CRITICAL MASS 2

COVID influenced some choices and changes made by some athletes and some people in certain businesses concerning their life goals or careers.
We now give you,
"Critical Mass 2"
Some people can play in a safe dome, others cannot, and gotta stay home. COVID is like big, drifting, blowing snow. It's a cold covering all, and nowhere to go. Schools had a very crazy thirst for football to be the best and first.

The intense, cool basketball coach was the easiest to approach. I hit hard every book, basically that's all it took. They wanted me to ball; some really believe that was all. Playing sports and doin' anatomy can be a very wide dichotomy. In this mad hot sports scene, you gotta be Uber clean. My solemn, quiet, nerdy style suits me like a good science lab trial. Keepin' your head above water is the most important starter. It's about using your downtime to make that uptown dime.

Wanna stack phat cheese, go hard with no quit, please. Any

career can make you grow, and all your peeps will glow

Willpower is what you use to keep you from the blues. Being idle, staying safe, and such, is not doin' way too much.

Any comments or questions for our mental health therapist, or information on chapter 4 back story can us an email.

Thanks
parentsproductions2025@yahoo.com

CHAPTER 5

CRITICAL MASS 3

The snow can be unbearable and brutally cold, while COVID can be bawdy and badly bold.
COVID has got so many families distraught, COVID disrupted businesses, and people got caught.
COVID changed and derailed careers, and some people are now in the arrears.
COVID has caused depression, and COVID has wreaked havoc in the medical profession.
COVID is a worldwide serial killer, truly, ain't nothin' more realer.

COVID is a mindless life-stealer,
like a poker-cheatin' dealer.
COVID is colder than minus
zero, but COVID is going to
meet our hero.
COVID is for real, cold-blooded,
and COVID is going to be
stunted.
COVID is a serious, stone-cold
killer, and COVID grinds up
people like a Miller.
COVID is way too lame, had to
switch up my life game.
Time now to get business tame
with the CEO by my last name.
Gotta be a Jack-of-All-Trades
and use them like fencing blades.

Rockin' straight tailor-mades
'til the CoVid killer fades.
These times will get better with
a peer-reviewed paper and
letter.
Then we'll hit the floor like a
smooth stepper, with vaccines
and therapeutics as a helper.
On one day, wear a flower to
show solidarity power for every
father and mother.
Every sister and brother, every
friend and lover, who are now
under the Creator's cover.
No time to be laid back, lax,
they paid the ultimate life tax.
Unfortunate is the bare fact
that Bubbles and no fans lack.

We're nearing a safe harbor to take CoVid to the barber, to beat the Coronavirus core, in this unseen, deadly war.

Any comments or questions for our certified mental health therapist or chapter 5 back story can be sent to an email.

Thanks
parentsproductions2025@yahoo.com

CHAPTER 6

CRITICAL MASS 4

Introduction
People should not allow setbacks to overshadow their main objective of excelling in any sport or career. We now give you,
"Cee Cee"
Anyone doing sports of any kind should not let COVID put you in a bind.
Cee Cee is not my name; rhyming is not my game. A dope Rapper I'm not, and I didn't puff pot. I was a clean nineteen, with no mean gang scene.

Twenty years ago, my mom gave me a good life. Now, COVID gives all some kind of strife.

Everyone knows COVID is contagious, and it became totally outrageous. All people know that COVID is not an addiction. COVID is horrible, and you can't make a prediction. COVID does not get likes, and the sickness bites.

Being a puffed-out stoner can make you an outcast loner. Therefore, I definitely had to pass on the exotic green gas. My mom can rest in peace, the COVID killer did cease. Had to step outside my peer box, with my willpower and no detox.

In any promising career, it is best to put rec-weed in the rear.

Any questions or comments for our certified mental health therapist or the back story on chapter 6 back story can send us an email.

Thanks
parentsproductions2025@yahoo.com

CHAPTER 7 CRITICAL MASS FIVE

CAUGHT-UP ONE

Not one TV ad, it's oh so sad, from word of mouth, you may go south. How fast the spread, to spend your bread. Bacca is back and on the attack.

Floodin' BaccaWoods in all neighborhoods. In one whole year, puffin' with your peer, you can blow more than a stack on something totally Wack. It won't get you high, but you just might die.

It's a cryin' shame, puffing on something lame. Life is never a game, these old days are not the same.

Bacca is like a runaway train. It comes at you like acid rain

Many know the pain that they cannot contain. Tars and Nicotine can make people fiend. Please do not ever start, or you could be on a cart. Bacca is a no-life game that no one can tame, also where no one can win. It will take out your family or friend.

Any comments or questions for a certified mental health therapist or chapter 7 back story send us an email.
Thanks
parentsproductions2025@yahoo.com

CHAPTER 8

"BENJI AND DAVON"

HOPE CAN STOP ALL THE CRIME
WITH A MEANINGFUL COOL RHYME.
IT'S BEEN FAR TOO LONG TO MAKE A SENSIBLE, WORKABLE WAY
TO STOP ALL THE CARNAGE AND CHAOS SOMEDAY.
I'M FROM THE CHI
WHERE SOME PEOPLE DO DIE,
LOTTA PEOPLE DO CRY.
CHI-TOWN FOR SURE IS NOT THE ONLY PLACE
CITIES ACROSS THE NATION SHARE THAT SAME SPACE.

A PROMISING UNFULFILLED LIFE
CAN CREATE A WHOLE LOTTA STRIFE,
IT CUTS LIKE A DOUBLE-EDGED KNIFE. HURTS CHILDREN AND SOMEBODY'S WIFE.
BENJI AND DAVON PASSED AWAY FAR TOO SOON,
EACH TAKEN OUT BY UNCARING GOONS
USING A COUPLE OF GUNS THAT KILLED SOMEONES' SONS.
BENJI AND DAVON COULDA MADE SOMETHING NEW
FOR ME AND YOU AND THE WHOLE WORLD TOO!!!

BENJI AND DAVON COULDA SPIT A SOCIETY CHANGING RAP TUNE.
THEIR LIFE WILL NEVER BE A FUNNY CARTOON.
CHI-TOWN BROUGHT OUT SO MANY FEARS,
BENJI AND DAVON WAS GONE IN A SHORT 18 YEARS, BRINGING TO MANY, MANY TEARS
THAT CUTS LIKE THE SHARPEST OF SHARP SHEARS.
HOPE CAN STOP ALL THE CRIME WITH A COOL DOPE RHYME, IT'S BEEN FAR TOO LONG
TO KEEP HEARING THE SAME OLD SONG.

WE MUST MAKE A SENSIBLE, WORKABLE WAY, TO STOP THE UNWANTED CARNAGE AND CHAOS SOMEDAY.

ANY QUESTIONS, AND COMMENTS FOR OUR CERTIFIED MENTAL HEALTH THERAPIST, OR CHAPTER 8 BACK STORY, CAN SEND US AN EMAIL

THANKS
parentsproductions2025@yahoo.com

ABOUT THE AUTHOR:

BORN AND RAISED IN CHICAGO, IL, UNTIL 1969. WORKED AND VISITED FROM NEW YORK, NY, TO FLORIDA ON THE EAST COAST. FROM SAN FRANCISCO TO SAN DIEGO ON THE WEST COAST. FROM MINNESOTA, DETROIT, AND CHICAGO IN THE MIDWEST. FROM ARKANSAS AND MISSISSIPPI IN THE GULF COAST AREA. WENT TO SCHOOL IN ARKANSAS AND GEORGIA
VIETNAM ERA VETERAN

www.ingramcontent.com/pod-product-compliance
Lightning Source LLC
Chambersburg PA
CBHW050249010526
44107CB00003B/247